Frannie Loves Her Postman

Written by Lisa Laskey
Photographs and Layout by Lisa Laskey

Graphic Design by Vicki Burke
https://www.facebook.com/VickiBurkeAuthor

#frannielife

To Frannie Joy,
for showing us what love really looks like

Hi, my name is Frannie...

... and this is Postman Dan.

I've been running out to see him
since my love for him began.

The reason that I run to him
is simple you will see,

It's to show him that he really is quite special to me.

I wait everyday to see and to kiss him,

I stare out the door to be sure I won't miss him.

He brings us our mail,
stops his truck for a minute...

and when I run out, I sometimes jump in it.

I watch and I wait for him to stop by,

Then I rush out the door so he'll lift me up high.

I run in the summer, I run in the fall...

But most rainy days, I won't run at all.

I hate how it feels when it's wet on the ground,

I start to walk out,

then I turn back around.

How on earth will I see him,

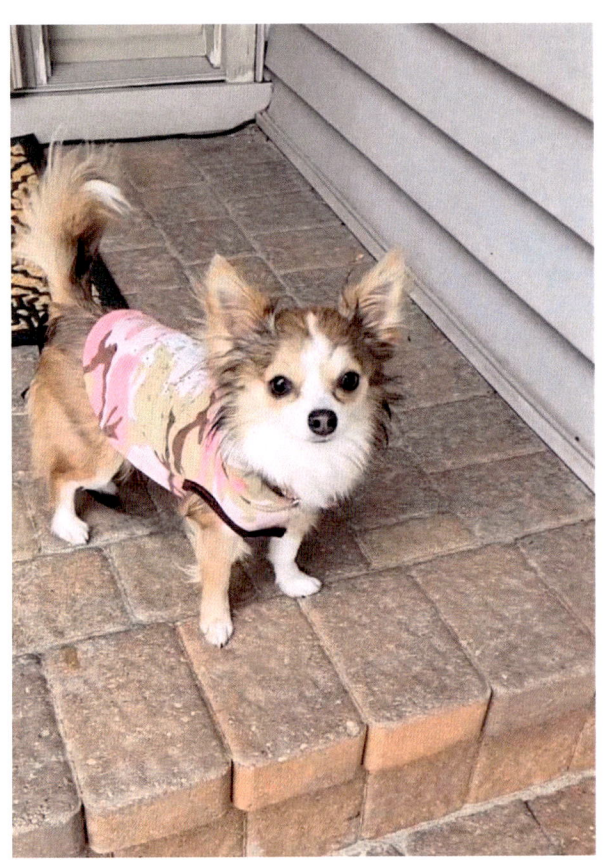

I can't move ahead,

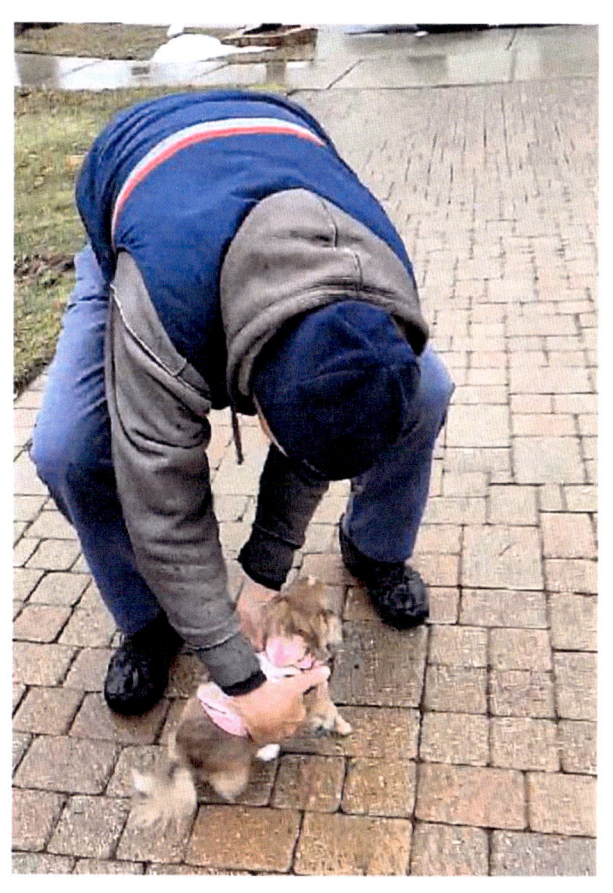

But surprise!
Postman Dan comes to me instead.

17

On bright sunny days, I run in a hurry.

I rarely go out when there's snow or a flurry.

The ice on the ground is too much to bear...

**Postman Dan comes to save me,
he really does care.**

Some days I run out to him off to the side,

But he'll come get me,

on his shoulder I ride.

I love how he holds me so close to his chest,

And that's just one reason that I love him best.

I've run to him almost three years and that's plenty.

I think I've run more than one thousand and twenty.

Mom says my run count is not quite that high,

It's more like four hundred and seventy five.

So many runs to the one I adore,

And because I love him, I'll run so many more!

And when he retires

and my run days are done,

I hope to have loved him ten thousand and one!

The End

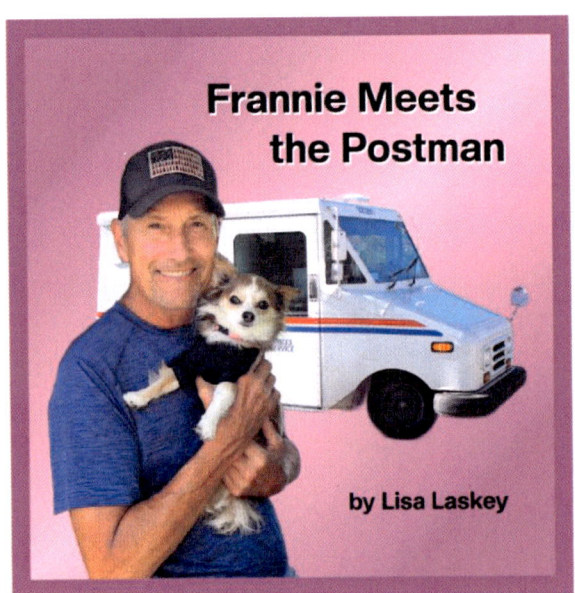

Frannie Meets the Postman

by Lisa Laskey

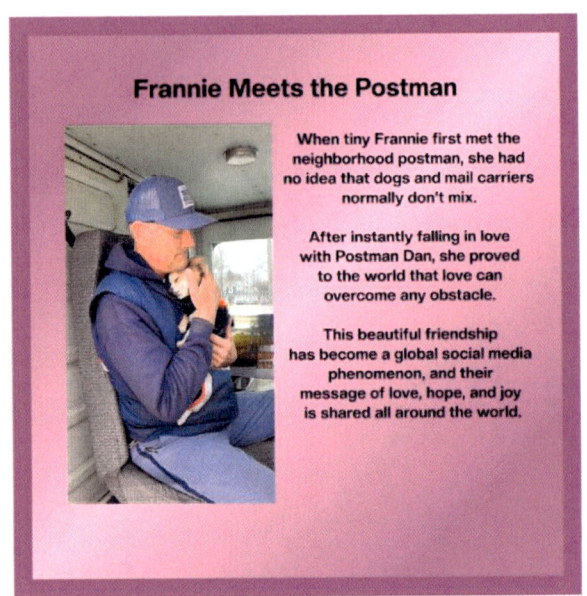

Frannie Meets the Postman

When tiny Frannie first met the neighborhood postman, she had no idea that dogs and mail carriers normally don't mix.

After instantly falling in love with Postman Dan, she proved to the world that love can overcome any obstacle.

This beautiful friendship has become a global social media phenomenon, and their message of love, hope, and joy is shared all around the world.

You may also enjoy the first two books in the "FranDan" series, "Frannie Meets the Postman" and "Frannie's Favorite Kiss."

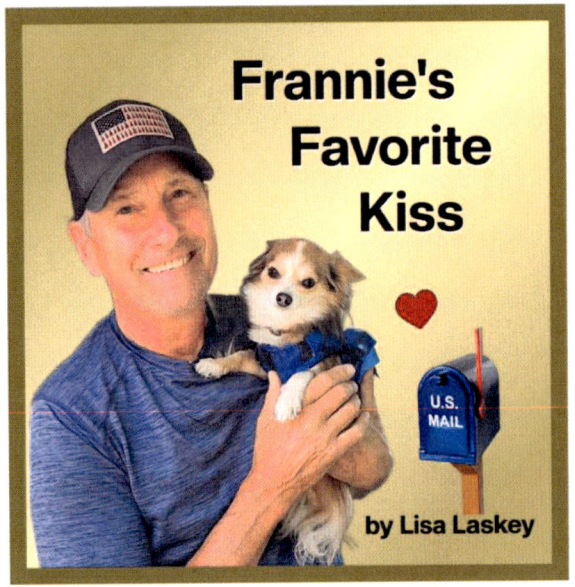

Frannie's Favorite Kiss

by Lisa Laskey

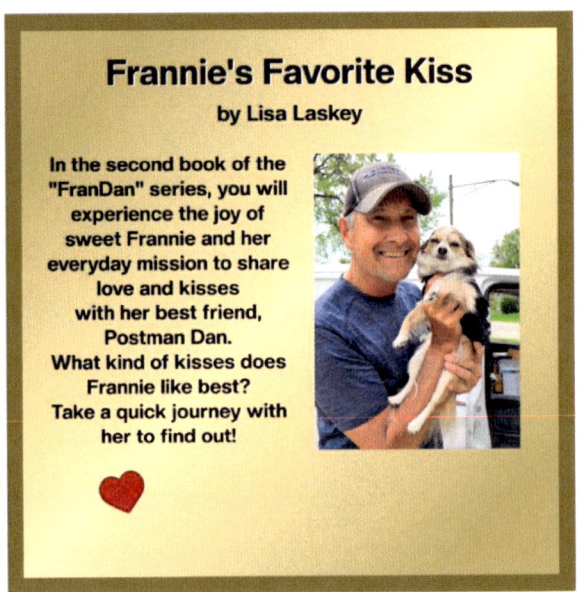

Frannie's Favorite Kiss

by Lisa Laskey

In the second book of the "FranDan" series, you will experience the joy of sweet Frannie and her everyday mission to share love and kisses with her best friend, Postman Dan. What kind of kisses does Frannie like best? Take a quick journey with her to find out!

Frannie Nation

Thankful for the Love and Generosity of the Frannienation Community

From all of us to all of you
Thank you, Frannienation

About the Author

Lisa Laskey is a gifted musician, artist, videographer, and digital creator.

After adopting her very special pup, Frannie Joy, in September of 2021, she realized she could use her artistry skills to share the loving friendship of Frannie and Postman Dan with others through social media. The Fran-Dan story quickly gained attention from millions of viewers, and the Frannienation community was born.

Today, the "FranDan" love story brings smiles to many people around the world, reminding us all that true love and friendship can be found even in the most unusual circumstances.

Lisa and her husband Dwayne have 2 sons and currently reside in the NW suburbs of Chicago with their sweet Frannie Joy.

All of Lisa's videos can be found on these social media links :

Facebook: https://www.facebook.com/lisa.laskey.5
Instagram: https://www.instagram.com/frannielife.dog
Tiktok: https://www.tiktok.com/@lisaandfrannie
Youtube: https://www.youtube.com/@LisaandFrannie